Copyright © 2024 by K.M. Jace.

All rights reserved. No part of this book may be reproduced in any form or by any electronic or mechanical means, including information storage and retrieval systems, without permission in writing from the publisher, except by reviewers, who may quote brief passages in a review.

This publication contains the opinions and ideas of its author. It is intended to provide helpful and informative material on the subjects addressed in the publication. The author and publisher specifically disclaim all responsibility for any liability, loss, or risk, personal or otherwise, which is incurred as a consequence, directly or indirectly, of the use and application of any of the contents of this book.

MILTON & HUGO L.L.C.
4407 Park Ave., Suite 5
Union City, NJ 07087, USA

Website: www.miltonandhugo.com
Hotline: 1-888-778-0033
Email: info@miltonandhugo.com

Ordering Information:
Quantity sales. Special discounts are available on quantity purchases by corporations, associations, and others. For details, contact the publisher at the address above.

Library of Congress Control Number:	2024926050
ISBN-13: 979-8-89285-406-1	[Paperback Edition]
979-8-89285-407-8	[Hardback Edition]
979-8-89285-408-5	[Digital Edition]

Rev. date: 12/02/2024

VERSIONS OF OURSELVES

Table of Contents

Introduction 1
PAST 19
PRESENT 35
FUTURE 61

Introduction

We haven't been properly introduced
even though I've known you all my life,
But it's finally time to meet myself

Written

She's written in many fonts,
with different handwritings

Scribbled across many *pages*,
This time she holds the pen

She's a collection of stories,
adventures and tragedies

Wait until you read the series,
words she never was able to speak
until they were on paper

<u>Missing</u>

I'm still finding *myself*,
But I know she's close by

She's missing in the shadows
of the past,
But I'm going to bring
her home safe

I'll show her the love
that the past never gave us,
A love we don't have to earn

Little does she know
what the future holds
And I can't wait to show her

Life

It belongs to me now,
What beautiful things
I'm going to fill it with

Many times I wanted to let it go,
But now I've won

Of course it's still not easy,
but where's the fun?
Only I can hold myself back

My life belongs to me
A journey unfiltered and filled with love
Watch me finally be free

Pages

You are a story
with many pages.
Some spilled with ink,
some remaining blank

How many of your own
have you read?
How many have you shared?

It's okay to still be afraid,
Letting your inner monologues
be in your story for others to grow

But what's a book
if its never read?
A secret even to you, the author

Reflection

When was the last time
you looked yourself
in the eye?

Allow yourself to dig through
the emotions you buried?
The marks of a life
still being lived?

Don't you want to see
your progress?
The reflection of a story
not told with words

Don't let regret win,
It'll erase your stories
Everyone deserves
to be their own piece of art

Prepare

Get ready to struggle
Get set to thrive
Go invent yourself

Be prepared to fail,
Your success will be
worth it

I will master my own potential,
no matter what it takes
I deserve all of my wins

No one can take
what I've given myself,
No matter the hard work

This chapter I will give
myself everything
I was ever rejected

<u>Versions</u>

They all matter
the ones you're proud of,
the ones you're ashamed of

Only you have seen them all,
all the versions of yourself
that made you into the
story that you are

Eras of error,
chapters of bliss,
segments of experience

Some are missed
Others even hidden by pain
Let now's version hold them
close and safe

Layers

So many scattered pages,
words written with a pen
You never held

Stories of your past,
barely remembered
but the book belongs to you

Layers of shame,
regrets that stain
your reflection

To have never written
for yourself is terrifying
but now's the *chance*

You're a draft
now free to truly make
your layers your own

Erase

It's okay to be scared.
To erase what others wrote
to keep you invisible

But it's not your truth
the future is a new chance
but your past still deserves a goodbye

Of course its not easy
to be haunted by
your own ghosts

Flickers of regrets
mingling in rediscovery,
A personal war

Never forget the strength
you've always carried,
especially when it's all you had

Trying

Of course it isn't easy,
that's why you keep it
to yourself

Learning to be present,
healing from the past,
trying to grow the future
all at once

Shame fights you daily
that's when you fall *silent*
and disappear into its
cold familiar arms

Some days are harder
then others to bring yourself back,
but you somehow always do

Trying is hard,
failure is not a option
even if all you want to do is compare

Enough

I know its hard to believe
but you still matter
even if you don't feel enough

Comparison holds you hostage,
regret eats you alive
drowning in your own self disgust

But enough is *enough*
why be your cruelest critic
when you can be your
biggest supporter

Imagine being able to present
your best self and not shy
from the mirror

Someone from nothing,
becoming everything they
ever wanted

Chapters

Welcoming a new chapter,
A developing version,
this time I get to know her

Finally no need to rush,
restrictions of opinions
no longer in control

I can't wait to show her home,
There hasn't been a place
called that in a long time

Life is finally up to us,
A promise finally kept to word
What a chapter this will be,
We're safe now

<u>End</u>

How strange it is
to feel a chapter
close

Goodbye's left unsaid,
Perhaps for the best
Now I'm free

But the transition can't
be overlooked
Can you believe you thought
You wouldn't make it this far?

For too many years
I begged for a ending,
Then it came without closure

Finally there's a beautiful
beginning,
This time I'm the writer

Stuck

I'm no longer where I was,
everything I wanted to love
was always wrong

Even time to myself
had to be snuck,
always having an illusion
of choice

I finally belong to myself
only I can keep me on track,
the work won't be done for me

The past likes to keep you stuck,
promising what's familiar
But those darkest days also
brought promises to yourself

Don't let them go to waste

Promise

I didn't think I would
make it this long...
but I made myself a promise

Only I got me through
those darkest days,
too many still not remembered

Reliability had to come
from me,
A work ethic that takes no breaks

Endless trials of disappointment,
fighting my abundance of
persistence

I'll never forget what I never had,
But the promises to myself
Have no intentions of failure

PAST

A forced adult in a child's body,
Absorbing the stress of everyone else
like a sponge until it became her own
I promise to love her the way
she always needed

Steps

Falling is okay,
Just don't forget to stand back up

Be mindful of the progress
A silent teacher of its own

Be cautious of the steps,
Someone else will use them someday

Falling is inevitable,
Just remember to celebrate another try

<u>More</u>

More in *love*,
More in growth

More silencing my own demons,
Venomous whispers locked away
and shadowed by embracing
self love

More adventures,
Blooming memories that
dance with the ones of the past

More love of the future,
Proving that obstacles are
going to make the wins
even sweeter

Yesterday

You made it,
Even when you thought
you wouldn't

How beautiful is that?
Another chapter
completed

To have a yesterday
no one has experienced
like you

A new layer of good and
bad memories to mold
the works of your today
and tomorrow

Lost

For so long she was limited
to herself
Shaped to be *perfect*
For others

If she was good at everything
she had value.
But she was lost to herself

Constant striving to
be better,
Burt she was always drowning

How good she got at hiding
the struggles that
she saw as weakness

Creation

For so long you were shaped
by others
Molded only to fit their needs

Now your own history
is a blur to you,
But here you stand

So much you had to hide away
Be silent. Be perfect.
Don't let your own needs get
in the way

Finally it's *time*
Become a creation of
your own design

Let yourself be shaped
By your own
Love

<u>Once</u>

Once you were nothing
but uncertain,
Everyday a new struggle
to overcome

Once you had a list of reasons
to quit,
Motivation to push through
becoming harder and harder

It wasn't fair,
To live life so long like that.
Once was *enough*

But now you're doing it,
Still pushing for that once
In a lifetime life.
And it'll be worth it

<u>Lonely</u>

For the longest time
you don't recognize
how loud silence can be

Once silence was a luxury,
A small break from the
yelling you still flinch from

And then there was
just the quiet,
And soon even that
became too loud

How do you identify
loneliness when
you're so used to being alone?
You welcome in love...

<u>Always</u>

What depth it carries,
the word "always"
used as a positive and
a negative

But where do you focus it?
How easy it is to get *lost*
in how cruel it can be

Always messing up
Always a burden
Always a work in progress

But the narrative
Can be changed,
If you let yourself

Always improving
Always learning
Always deserving to be here

Her

She's safe now
I wish I could tell her that,
my inner child

No one will ever know
How strong she had to be
at all times

Abuse came in many forms,
I'm proud of her for
keeping her kindness

How starved she was for love,
always thinking
it has to be earned

She finally finds it,
A love that's here to stay
She finally won

Almost

I was almost good enough,
years lost trying to please
Losing myself before I even
could learn who I was

How much farther I could
Have been in life had I
been in my own control...

Fear is a powerful prison,
shame keeps me in my own jail
but I know I'm almost out,
Adventures I crave almost in hand

Comparison is my enemy
now that I'm starting from scratch
but I know she's almost there,
The me I desperately want
to come home to.

<u>Before</u>

Screaming was communication
Love was earned
To relax was to be lazy

So many times I almost broke
my silence
Always telling myself "not yet"

Instead staying obedient
Before brought too much risk
Now I don't have to fight

I wish I could tell my younger
self how proud I am of her,
of remaining strong even when silenced

She never even got to be
A child,
But now she's safe

Silent

Once I made the mistake of speaking up,
but I'm a fast learner
To be seen and not heard kept me safe

Always be obedient
Make sure to be silent
Your value lies in how you work

Now my voice is gone
Internal screams left to whispers
Endless terrors of mistakes

I didn't't mean to lose myself
I promise to protect her better,
Just another chance

One day she'll hear her laugh
No longer caged in silence
What a beautiful journey
that'll be...

Survive

I lost my childhood having to
grow up too fast,
A child left to take care of her
caretakers

She barely learned how to
care for herself,
Others always came first

I can't believe we survived,
Clinging to the shards of our heart
Being naive kept us kind

Now there's nothing to escape from,
How do I tell my nervous system that?
There's finally a future to see...

Done

I will always hold gratitude,
so much I couldn't yet do alone
But then I learned

And then I remembered,
how often your words left
me sobbing on then floor

You taught me how to be strong
But I also mastered how to live
in fear

Never feeling like a child
but a machine and a puppet
How long did you expect me
to stay that way?

I'm finally done,
It hurts to not get a goodbye
But my life belongs to me now

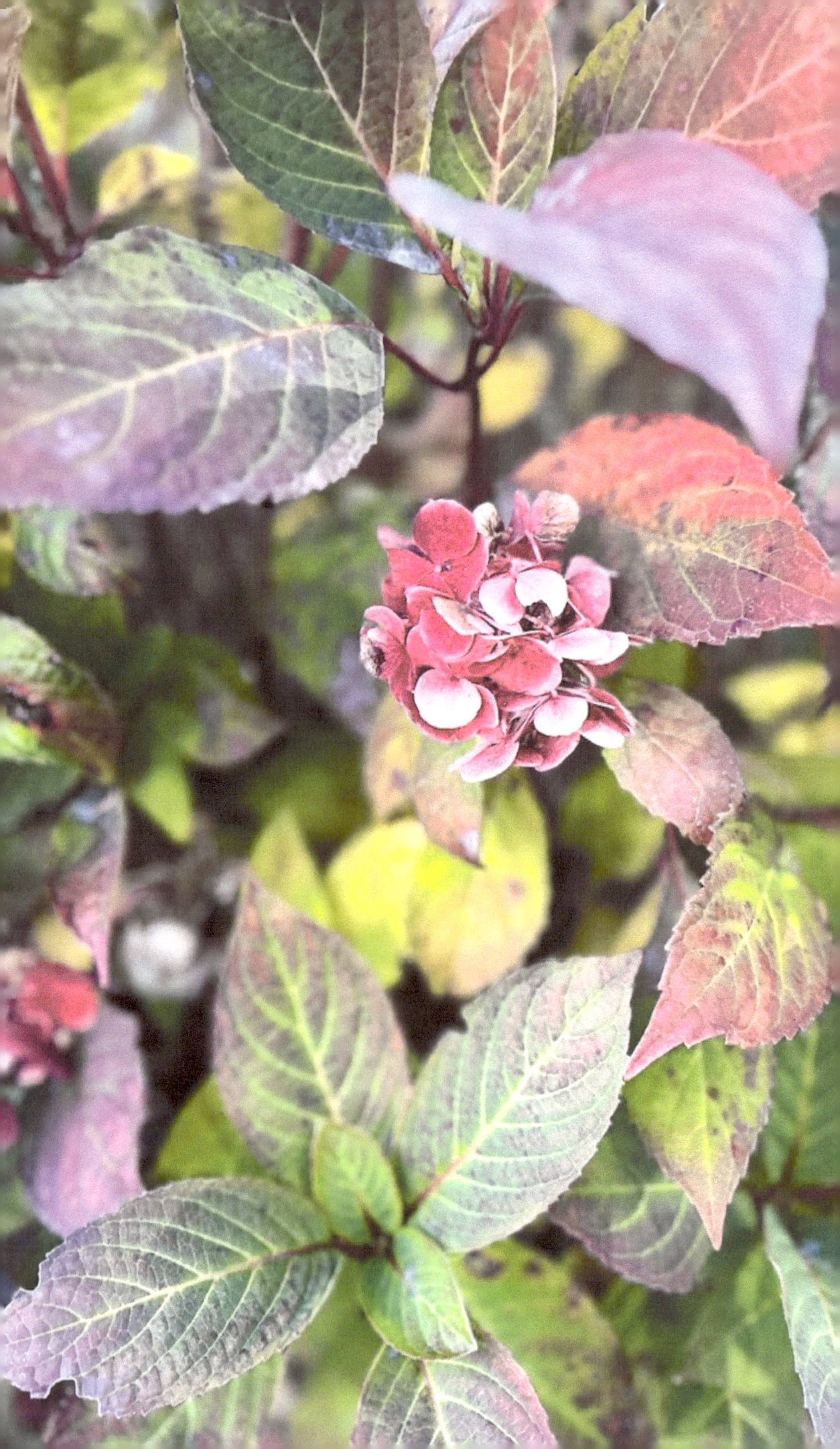

PRESENT

I've never lived for me before,
how does one become themselves
When they never expected
to live this long?
I suppose now is the time to learn...

Chance

The need for change
brought the chance
for more

The need for a chance
to keep growing,
Building the peace once
refused

Chances are it'll fail,
Crumble just as its reached
Worth the risk should it
Succeed

Life's too short to
have no risks to chance
imagine the stories
you'll tell

Today

What a adventure
It is for a new day,
a new story for your book

Chores and routines
Someday you could miss
the mundane

Today wasn't written
in stone,
Don't forget to fill it
with your magic

Make today a gift
for your
tomorrow

Love

You truly don't know it
until you feel it,
A welcoming embrace

Crazy how it can come
Out of nowhere...
Bringing back your fire

It's scary to let it in,
But when you do...
What adventures you'll have

When it's done right
of course it takes work.
Even when life keeps being cruel,
Love is there to be
your peace

__Growth__

It isn't easy
It definitely isn't fair,
Having to heal what hurt you...

But what power you'll have
when the love pieces together
the brokenness

That growth becomes
the real you,
And only some get to see

Sure it'll take time,
but it'll be worth it
Especially when you see
how you glow

Limit

Notice yourself
It's okay to slow down
If you rush, are you
even living?

Limits make you human,
It gives you a place
to rest

It's not a end,
Just a place to grow

You're not a machine
but a living piece of art
Never let your darkness
say otherwise

Found

Then she had *enough.*
What was she worth
to herself?

Her silence spoke volumes
But then she found
her voice

For too long
she didn't matter
to herself

The purity of love
saved her,
A new value of self
found from inside

New

Everything is different
this time,
Fears and thrills align

Burt this chapter feels like
my own,
Finally a new experience

Now what?
Now I find myself through
the cracks of somebody
else's vision

I'm my biggest prize,
Covered in a new
layer of self love

Alone

No one tells you
how scary it is
to let people in

After so many years
being able to only rely
on yourself

Alone has always been
safe
Until being alone becomes
your prison

Being ashamed of your
own solitude,
Afraid to seek
connection

How powerful you become
when you let love in

Practice

It's okay to not know,
to be behind others.
But you still shame yourself

What's the fun of taking
the path of everyone else?
Practice loving your own

Do you really want to bury
yourself in the achievements
of others?

The temptations to be like
everyone else,
the inner disappointment of being yourself

Learning how to be safe
as yourself and not ashamed
Practice makes perfect

<u>Wandering</u>

They never quit,
The thoughts that only
Hurt

The whispers of doubt
spoken in your own voice
that only you can hear

Even in times of bliss
they wander,
Silencing you into uncertainty

Some days are louder
then others
But will you let the
wandering love take
its place?

Priority

You forgot didn't you?
That you've always been
a priority

You lost track of the years,
Being told that your best
has never been enough

Always told that your worth
only comes from what
you can do for others

You can't pour
from a empty cup

Don't you remember?
You're the main character
of your own story
Prioritize it

Enter

Can you believe it?
Here you are in this new chapter,
entering a peace you've
always dreamed about

Fear and guilt within
a new territory,
Yet hope and excitement
for this adventure

Now you can enter
A sense of self that once
wasn't safe to explore

Lighting lamps
in the shadows of your mind,
Speaking love to your
whispers of self hatred

Never

It belongs to me
The peace I lost to screams
The adventures lost to control

It has always belonged to me
Once I didn't know that,
Other hands took control first

Never again will I speak
in whispers of fear,
I direct myself now

No one tells you how hard
it is to trust again,
Let alone yourself

But when life finally is in your
own hands...
It's worth the chance

Experience

It's never been a race
but it's always felt like it,
Milestones you have yet
to reach

Feeling trapped in the
years of your past self
Plagued with shame

Wanting to experience life
But starting from far too many
steps behind

How easy it is to lose
your sense of value
Against the accomplishments
of everyone else

Never forget the promise
to give yourself the everything
you've always wanted

Loud

Silence is a luxury,
One that my mind refuses
to experience

Endless conversations
nobody else can hear,
when does it stop being so loud?

Wanting to celebrate my progress
all I do is overanalyze,
How do I stop ?

Do I love or hate myself?
Do I even let others love me?
Of course I became my own bully

No wonder I'm always tired
yet can never rest,
But I won't let myself punish me
into success...

<u>Lingering</u>

It's all here
and it drowns me.
The storms of my mind
trapping me in my mistakes

Rarely is there silence,
yet I crave it
No one knows how *loud* it is
as I sit alone

The lingering traumas
have a lot to say
But they're not welcome

I will make myself my home,
But will I allow myself
to deserve it?

For the future I now crave,
I will make sure of it

Expectations

Whose standard do I hold
myself to?
For too long my life was not
my own

How lonely it is to grown up
where love had to be earned
Yet never being able
to meet expectations

If only I could give back
This new found love a piece
to my younger self...

But now I'm making
her *proud*
And loving her with softness
that we finally found

Noise

To be present in the moment
is such a gift,
My thoughts give no peace

To be able to relax with
those I love most,
But I can't quiet my mind

Unlimited noise of
insecurities and failures,
Striving for unattainable
perfection

I just want to be happy
with myself,
Yet I keep thinking
I didn't earn that

So much noise in my head,
How do I make it
positive?

Nothing

I've always been good at
having nothing
But I've never been proud
of it

Even things I give myself
feel like they can vanish,
Gifts were tools of punishment
after all...

But to remain grateful
has been my power,
even when envy whispers

Now everything has changed
and only I stand in my way
I always come back from nothing
But this time I'll give myself everything

Terrified

I can't stop, or won't
Because it never goes away,
Constant reminders of
past failures

What if I never find success?
What do I even define as success?
Do I want it for myself or others?

I'm terrified that I'll never
be happy with myself
But don't I deserve to make
myself proud?

I fear the work will never stop
Filled with fantasies of living life
as I watch the world do it for me
One day I hope to master both

Disgust

Nobody can dislike me like I can,
Growing up never being good enough
seems to stick with you for awhile...

When is it my turn to look in
the mirror and be proud of
who I see?

Being lost in your own loneliness,
Wishing you could connect
like everyone else

Can self love even heal
the self disgust?
When can I see my progress
take shape?

I can't let my trauma win,
Not when I worked this hard
to escape

Search

Who am I now that there's no one
telling me how to be?
Layers of myself being suppressed
for so long they've been scared to surface

Only when completely alone
can I even meet them
How I envy those who have made
home's within themselves

I'm so tired of searching
But buried deep down...
I'm still in there

Will I ever not be afraid
to disappoint myself?
I know that she's scared
But I promised her a magical life,
and I refuse anything less

Delay

There's always been a stranger
in my mirror...
A personality formed by others

Always enforced to be great
Never slowing down to process
Then it finally all stopped

Now I have a chance
to meet this stranger,
An introduction delayed
for far too long

She knows my deepest pains
Endured every attack in silence
But I'm scared she'll leave too

But she's always been there
and I refuse to disappoint her

Worth

A childhood left behind
A child raising her siblings
Always expected to pick up the slack

She learned fast
Worth had to be earned
It made her incredible
at taking abuse in silence

Her silence was her break
from screams she still hears,
Just once she wished she
screamed back

It shouldn't have been a life
that had to be survived
But she gave herself a second chance,
Worth belongs to her now

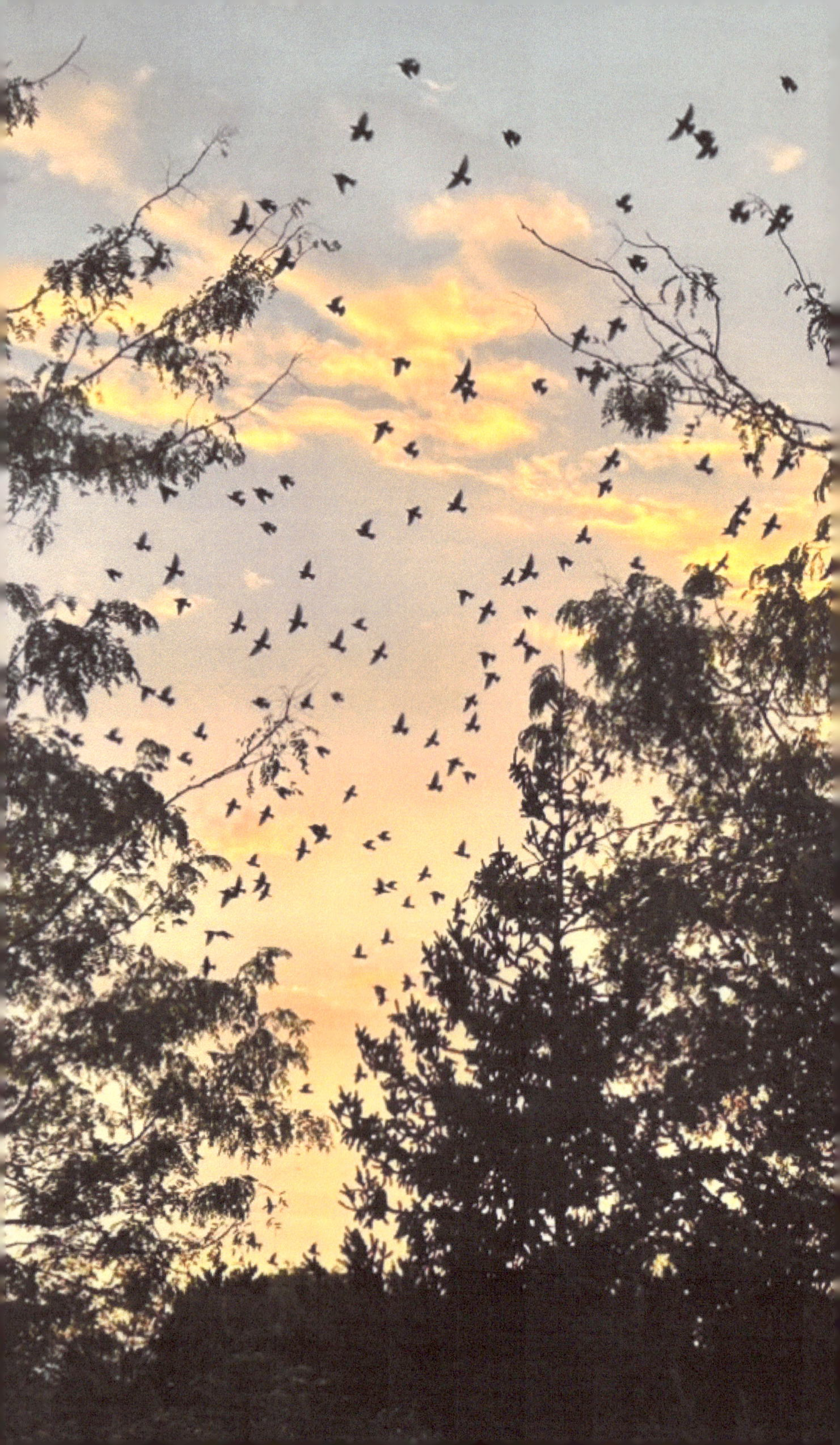

FUTURE

Once upon a time we didn't
imagine a future,
it was thought our death would
be by our own hand.
Digging ourselves out of
our own destruction
It's time to see what this future holds

Tomorrow

What a mystery
tomorrow brings,
A new chance
to create your story

How will you welcome it?
Even if it's not a
guarantee

Tomorrow isn't a promise,
But isn't that the
thrill?

To await a chance,
To add another chapter,
Even if its not promised

Time

Infinite, yet not enough
To slow down or
to haste

It's never been a promise,
What a gift that is
But make sure
not to waste it

What a journey
But be sure to enjoy the fast
among the slow

Time heals and wounds
How does something
invisible have such a
strong hold?

Make it count

Perfect

I know it's not real
But I want it.
The need for perfection

To be everything for
everyone,
But I skipped myself

Only finding my value
in my worth.
That's how I was taught

How do I love the flaws
and the scars?
A gentle kind of love
that I can only give to
myself

Proud

How many times have
your could nots become
you did?

All the times you
never asked for help
but still found success?

Surviving your storms
Basking in your sunshine
You should be proud

The struggles you never
let others see,
The wins you've kept
to yourself

Celebrate yourself
Keep making yourself
proud

Grateful

Once I thought I was done,
Done trying to survive
Done waiting for another
day to hurt

To leave would be easier,
But making the decision
to stay...
How worth it is was

Being grateful holds
more power now,
New memories that
could of never been

Don't rush the end,
Slow down the journey
The future belongs
to you too

Finally

There it is.
That light at the end
of the tunnel

That final shred of hope
once lost in the shadows
Finally found home

The peace to be in
the moment,
At first terrified
to feel so safe

Now you won't settle
for less
And to think you thought
you wouldn't make it this far…

Left

I didn't mean for it
 to be taken,
My sense of self

Endless years of being molded
into endless use for others,
My worth is for others

A flicker of courage
then discarded like nothing
Left as a shell

A book to be entirely
rewritten,
The *pages* are mine now

No one tells you how guilty
becoming yourself feels,
Erased words still leave indents

Less

No one tells you how isolating
it feels to become yourself
so late in life

What if you mess up?
Become even less then you
once were?

Belonging to yourself,
What a luxury that's terrifying
to lose again

You are yours.
Everyone deserves a redo
Becoming the love and guidance
you wish you always had

Less restriction and taunting
More growth and peace
By yourself
And for yourself

Acquired

I am a acquired taste
to myself,
A still in development version

How do I meet her
with kindness?
She deserves gentleness

Everyday is a new *reflection*
of personal introductions,
Evolving chances to make ourselves proud

How dare I be so critical
to someone who just wants
to be their best?

Soon not just a acquired taste,
But a welcome home

Enjoy

I forgot how to do it,
enjoy things,
or maybe I never learned

Always thinking I needed
to work harder
I have to earn the time

And yet I remain
dazzled by the things
that inspire me

Shades of art
finally stopping me
in my tracks

What magic it is
to create,
May it keep me in awe

<u>Mine</u>

My life belongs to me now
How I wish I could tell that to my younger self
She put up one hell of a fight
for so many years

We finally get to say no,
We finally get to slow down and enjoy
Small things often abused

This life is mine now
Scarred and scared but still standing
Finally being a priority

So much was never mine,
Even time a luxury
But now what do I do with it?
Every second feels so precious

Now go live them...

<u>Seen</u>

There's no such thing as perfection
Yet it's all I can think of
If I judge myself harshly,
I beat the world to the punch

Always fearing love will leave
just as I embrace it completely,
I'm supposed to be better then this

If I'm seen, how visible are my flaws?
But everyone has faults...
I still see mine as a burden

I wasn't meant to be here this long
Every day is a gift I fear to fail
I refuse to be my own worst enemy

Hopefully one day confidence
won't hurt to force...
I deserve to be here too

Closure

Sometimes you don't get
 a goodbye,
But the end was necessary

No one warns you about it,
the lingering guilt and shame
of putting yourself first

So many years of life lost
trying to earn an acceptance
As long as you follow orders

Inner peace is the real closure
Self made strength in knowing
no one will ever crush you like that again

Now you have to be earned
Never again will your time be wasted
You are your freedom

Dedication

This book was created from a lot of love, a lot of self-doubt and a lot of reassurance. Years were spent thinking of the ideas to combine words and nature to express an abundance of moments in life.

To my found family, thank you for being my rock when I wasn't sure if this project would ever take shape. You've been there through so many stages of my life and I never would have found my own confidence without your support.

To my partners, thank you for giving me the opportunity to experience love in its softest forms. You've gotten me out of my shell to take on life by the reins and make the most of each and every day with thrills and inspiration.

To my mom, thank you for from the very beginning always supporting my writing even if sometimes we didn't always see eye to eye. You kept that drive to write strong and now it's finally becoming a reality that I hope you're proud to see come to life.

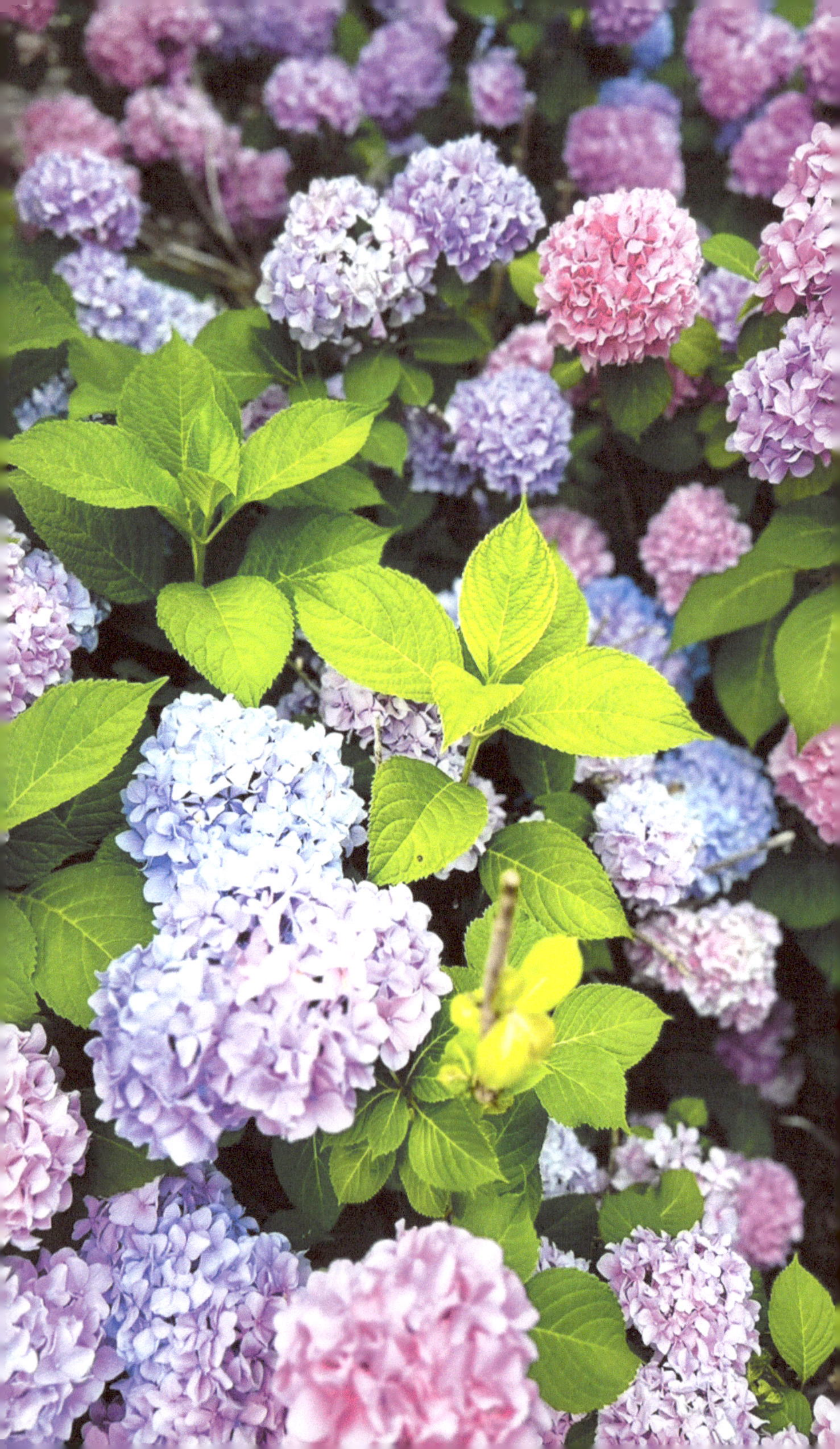